AF505636

F. Sherfey

THE SECRET SAGA OF FIVE SACK

So little is known about the life of Five-Sack that Mr. Reimers was forced to fill in many gaps from his own imagination, i.e., fiction, but the account in general is believed to be true. The material was taken from the Wes Lloyd manuscript but it also appears in an unpublished manuscript by Helga Travis of Prosser, Washington, entitled *Tumbleweed Trails*.

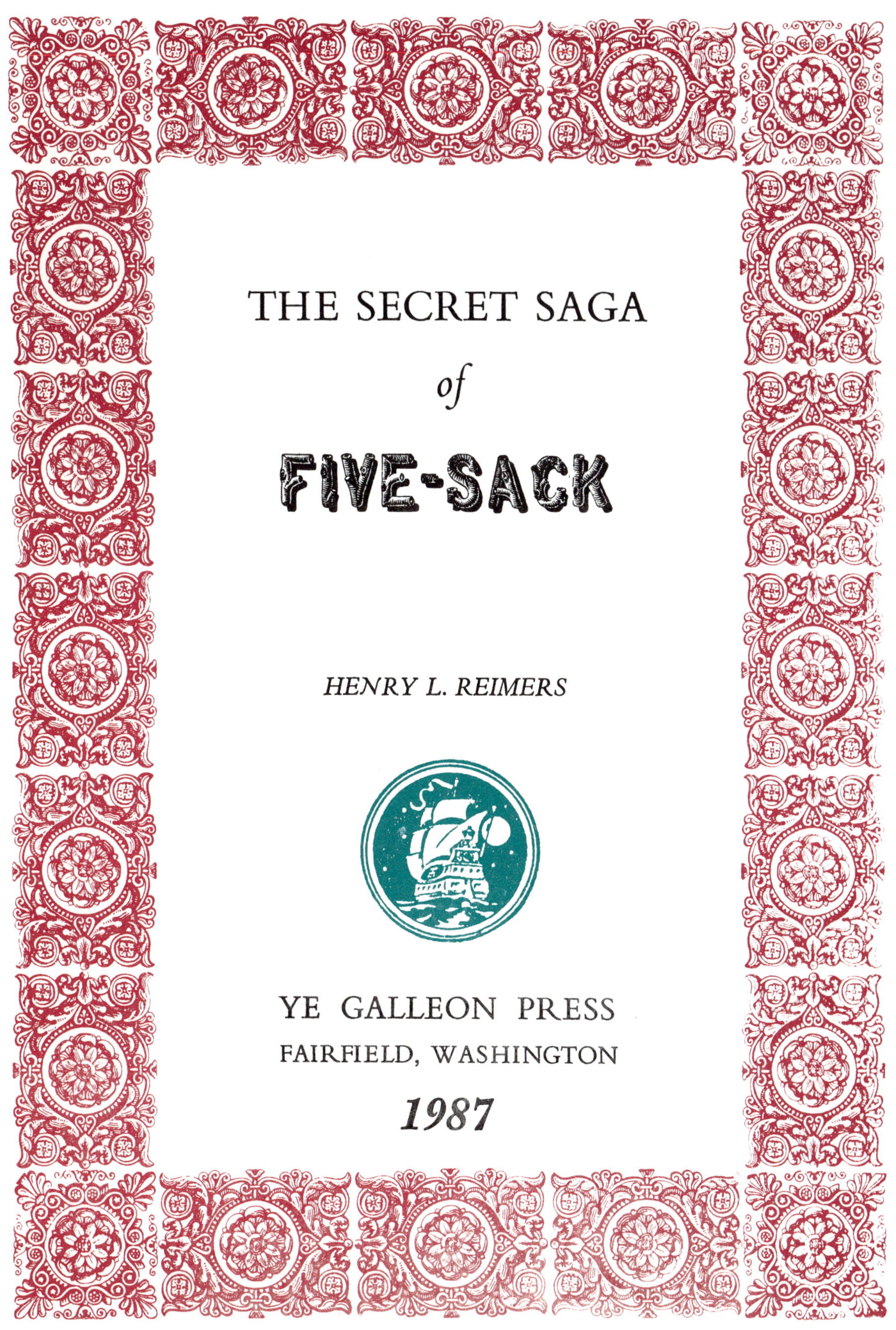

THE SECRET SAGA

of

FIVE-SACK

HENRY L. REIMERS

YE GALLEON PRESS

FAIRFIELD, WASHINGTON

1987

ISBN 0-87770-145-8

THE SECRET SAGA OF FIVE SACK

Five-sack, sometimes known as Five-star, was a Palouse Indian who proudly recalled an 1848 victory over the Oregon volunteers on the Touchet River, and the 1858 defeat of Colonel Steptoe at Rosalia. His fondest boyhood memory was of triumphant warriors returning to the junction of the Snake and Palouse rivers, confident the palefaces had been forever driven from their ancestral lands. The appearance of Chief Kamiakin represented the youth's closest association with fame, and the thrill lingered. That Colonel Wright and his soldiers later punished the villagers for their hostile acts should also have been kept in mind. Hub-deep ruts in the near-by Colville Trail as it approached Lyon's ferry suggested that "paths of peace" were replacing the older and more familiar ways. Possibly the dust stirred up by passing freight wagons obscured clear vision.

During the mid 1870's Five-sack's inmost yearnings were stimulated by news via "moccasin telegraph." War clouds hung low over the Wallowa Valley in northeastern Oregon. That land had been given to segments of the Nez Perce nation who wished to continue their ancient way of life, as opposed to more restricted agricultural life on a different reservation. Wallowa was certainly the most beautiful and ideal of regions, hallowed as a burial ground by generations of red men, whose claim to rightful ownership, previously confirmed by treaty, was now being contested.

The Nez Perces deserved justice from the United States government if ever gratitude belonged in national policy. When Lewis and Clark bogged down east of the Bitterroots, faced with failure and starvation, an aged tribesman named Toby guided the palefaces over Lolo Pass to sanctuary on the Clearwater. From there the journey to salt water was readily accomplished. Nez Perce were hospitable to 'mountain men' and missionaries, responding to the teachings of the Reverend and Mrs. Henry Harmon Spalding; and protected them during the Cayuse War. Tribesmen guarded Governor Isaac Ingalls Stevens during the Walla Walla Council of 1855, and Nez Perce ferried Steptoe's defeated forces across the Snake river after the Battle of Rosalia.

New faces on the national scene often overlook prior obligations, or are swayed by unexpected developments and the demands of expedience. The discovery of gold in Oregon and Idaho, plus the fact that lush grazing for Indian cattle and horses could be equally useful to white ranchers, brought matters to a crisis. Young Chief Joseph tried to pursue a course that would satisfy his restless followers and still gain some needed concessions from the government. There were numerous conferences with General Oliver Howard, whose attitude was strangely rigid and relentless when compared with his treatment of Apache leaders and raiders before and after this period. National representatives and Agency personnel pushed forward suggestions which violated provisions of the 1855 treaty which Joseph the Elder had trustingly signed with Isaac Stevens, particularly the provision that the Wallowa Valley in northeastern Oregon was to be given to Joseph and his band of Nez Perce Indians forever.

Such was the word hard riding Nez Perce emissaries carried to every Pacific Northwest tribe that had suffered in dealings with the "Great White Father." Joseph was resolute in his stand for peace but the young men clamored for war. Their plea was for help. Glory, spoils, a chance to avenge countless wrongs awaited the bold ones. When it was time to strike surely such famed warriors as White Bird, Yellow Bull, and Looking Glass would be with them. When the eloquent ambassadors to the Palouse nation rode away toward Spokane country they left behind one eager recruit.

Everything considered, Five-sack acted with restraint. First he joined a beef gather in the bunchgrass to the west. Indians frequently worked as cowboys and this round-up was urgent. The cattle were destined for delivery to General Howard's forces at Lapwai. Hollis Conover, well-known Waitsburg pioneer, in relating his experiences on the drive, described steamboats plying the Snake, laden with supplies and men for the Army. The need for reinforcements was soon evident.

When the beef herd was finally delivered at headquarters, soil was still moist on the graves of many soldiers who died during the futile battling on the slopes along the Clearwater. Efficient river transportation was providing personnel for the shattered ranks of General Howard. Five-sack alone arrived to hearten the equally hard hit following of Chief Joseph, on whose handsome, resolute features deeply-graven lines of care now added a sober dignity.

Well fed, if not especially well paid, adequately armed and mounted, the sturdy Palouse brave was more than a trifle disconsolate as he slipped away from his fellow drovers and sought Nez Perce Campfires. He had heard of raids in the Wallowa by "young men;" of cattle and horses lost during the retreat that then became advisable, of Indian victory at White Bird Canyon and forays in the Cottonwood region. Greatest of all had been the fierce fighting at the Clearwater, with an entire bluecoat army stopped in its tracks. Surely he was much too late; his warpath was over before it had begun.

Ensuing conversation with adults willing to share what was becoming common knowledge, however, revived his spirit. This war was far from over. Realizing it would be impossible to hold the chosen land, Joseph intended moving his stalwart folk to "buffalo country." This was territory known to all great warriors. For generations tribal bands, astride matchless Appalousas, had traveled Lolo Trail, engaging in bitter battles with Blackfeet who wanted no strangers hunting or raiding in Montana.

It was now late summer when the path should be in satisfactory condition. Buoyed by a number of faithful followers, trusting their dauntless courage, the young chief was confident of a safe, speedy journey to the hunting grounds once the rugged mountains were crossed. Non-combatants had already begun the march.

The Lolo Trail to this day is a grueling test for travelers, be they riders or drivers of motor vehicles. The route slants along steep slopes, descends deep saddles, balances on knife-edged ridges, skirts landslides when space can be found, and from the heights presents a view of interminable brushy highlands to the north. On the other side stark inclines drop to the canyon of the Lochsa River.

The wise tourist glues his eyes to ruts created by the travois poles of earlier wayfarers, or, if truly wise, elects to drive the scenic highway which follows a water grade parallel to the ancient passage. Forest fires have destroyed most of the large timber which was an obstacle to Joseph and his band. Down trees and windfalls were barriers which had to be cleared if there was no by-pass. As stages of the strenuous passage were completed hard working toilers re-created obstacles across the way, felling trees, rolling boulders and starting landslides wherever feasible.

A strong rear guard was posted and a nuisance force was detailed to keep the paleface troops under surveillance and to do everything possible that would delay organizing an immediate pursuit. Joseph's brother led this daring dozen and Five-sack was proud to be one of them. Hit and run dashes that stampeded the beeves, unsettled grazing horses and mules, and threatened the safety of teamsters whose freight hauls were so essential to the military were stimulating almost to the point of intoxication.

Experienced officers quickly responded to these gad-fly tactics and flung a series of patrols around the outer perimeter of the sun-scalded base, creating a challenge that was both perilous and inviting. Very shortly the Nez Perce "young men" were intercepted and scattered. Their spirited ponies carried them out of danger, convinced at last that it was now time to seek out and rejoin the kinsman who by now must be nearing Montana.

Five-sack was cut off from the others and his jaded animal was hard-pressed to match the speed of the grain fed cavalry horses as their riders fanned out on the flanks like hunting wolves. He was driven into a cul-de-sac, with no time to clamber out ahead of the bluecoats. He wheeled about to confront his captors, and thoughts of the great Kittitas Chief Owhi cornered in similar fashion by some of Col. George Wright's soldiers, brought him no feeling of confidence whatever. Words and a gesture from the enemy leader took the play out of his hands. Understanding well enough, he eased his rifle to the ground and one of the troopers took charge of it. Another gesture and he knew he was to follow the horsemen.

The laughing comments and jests of the group seemed strange to the Palouse partisan. These men had lost many comrades so far in the fighting. They should be angry with him, already regretful that he was a prisoner. Could it be that all of this funning was to make him think they were careless and off guard? Working with whites had given him insight to their attitudes and thinking to such an extent that he nudged his horse directly into the middle of those "laughers." They eyed him intently, but with a grudging glimmer of respect. It would be kinda hard to shoot him "while trying to escape," even if the "sarge" was looking yonderly with an intentness scarcely justified by the heat-seared landscape before them. As for Five-sack, the more soldiers they encountered the safer he felt though the situation remained little to his liking.

In the calaboose at Fort Lapwai the Palouse adventurer found the role of non-combatant decidedly irksome, as did a handful of non-treaty natives who had run afoul of the Military weeks earlier. Relief from confinement came when General Howard broke camp to take up pursuit of Joseph and his resolute tribesman. The relief however, was to another form of custody and seemingly endless travel. Well-guarded, the prisoners were packed into a stagecoach for a hot, dusty, humpty-dumpty dash to the steamboat landing at Lewiston.

Presently they were aboard a "fire canoe" which took them downstream between the Snake's towering bluffs, and past Five-sack's home village, which he eyed with a sense of foreboding. Once on the Columbia's robust current they passed the ruins of old Fort Walla Walla and at last reached a landing above Celilo Falls. The familiar sights, smells, and the sound of roaring, rushing waters which characterized the famous fishery were left behind as a lumbering wagon carried them over the rough portage road to The Dalles.

From there a steamboat transported them to The Cascades and a final portage, a good place once, in the days of the fur trade, but now the home of bluecoats without number, several of whom took over the duty of escorting the uneasy prisoners to Fort Vancouver. The next leg of their journey was on a large vessel to the stream's mouth, a rough crossing of the bar, and a sickening voyage parallel to the coast, during which none of the captives bothered to "count the suns,"—or worry about food.

At San Francisco there were a few days rest, probably in quarters at The Presidio, then rumbling steam cars, following the lead of an "iron horse," bore them up the Sacramento Valley to the vicinity of Sutter's Fort, well-known to the Northwest tribes a generation earlier. Here the tracks turned toward the rising sun to confront the challenging grades of the towering Sierra Nevadas.

It was good to finally leave that region of torturous climb, dizzying void, brake-shrieking descent, and line out for a clanking run across grim, but somewhat level deserts. Thereafter came an approach near the great lake of salt, over smaller mountains than the Sierras, along a sluggish river route through a country of prairies and monotonous plains.

At a station, apparently in Leavenworth, Kansas, the group transferred to other cars bound toward the Southwest, then followed more stagecoaching, succeeded by a close-curtained Army conveyance that traveled surrounded by vigilant cavalrymen. Tired as he was, the Palouse brave felt a thrill of pride. Could it be that he was "known?" Arrival at a bleak Oklahoma reservation left the question unanswered, but after the travel-worn prisoners were enrolled and somewhat adjusted to the routine of a changed way of life he continued to wonder.

To Agency officials responsible for too many rash, brash braves, traditional fighters all and worthy of strictest attention, the reluctant stranger from the Northwest posed no problem. They were "blind" and so knew nothing of the far place for which his heart yearned, nor that his inscrutable eyes envisioned there a cavalcade of dauntless warriors, their families, and their all, pressing persistently along a perilous winding path. Would it lead them to freedom?

It led them to a bleak Oklahoma reservation!

Five-sack was shocked by the poverty and desolation of Joseph's valiant band. In time he was able to learn the devastating circumstances of that tragic exodus, when survivors recognized he had once been an ally, a young man of the "nuisance" raiders. Downcast, for none of these former comrades appeared, he shared tobacco with older men — — and listened. Their words took him back to that day when the Nez Perce, realizing their lands were "lost," resolved on swift retreat over the Lolo Trail as the only solution for them and their ancestral way of life.

Several days of rugged trial brought the moving column to Lolo Creek. The people were worn and edgy. The horse herd was greatly reduced, for many animals came to grief along the cliffs. Others were tender-hoofed from the rocky going or gaunted by lack of forage and water. There was time for only a brief stay at the refreshing hot springs but soon a better sun would shine for Lolo Creek led to the rich Bitterroot Valley where grazing abounded. In near-by Missoula food supplies and ammunition would be plentiful. These Indians, with their tradition of friendship, had always been welcome customers at stores and trading posts. Suddenly they found their medicine "bad"!

Near the mouth of the valley they were descending a crude, hastily contrived fort barred the way. General Howard used a

THE SECRET SAGA OF FIVE SACK

"talking wire" and troops in Montana had been alerted to intercept the "hostiles." The resentful "young men" wanted to wipe out the stronghold but a cooler head prevailed. Joseph contented himself with "bluffing" an attack, and then led his "host" around the road-block, leaving it to revel in the satiric name of "Fort Fizzle."

This bloodless victory provided only temporary relief. Since the people of Missoula had shown such distrust the shortest way to "buffalo country" would surely be barred by bluecoats or once-friendly rifle bearing frontiersman. An alternative way would be long, south down the Bitterroot Valley, then by whatever path lay open.

Fiery, ambitious warriors presently saw action,—action aplenty. Some days later as the Nez Perce rested in camp a surprise attack by General Gibbon routed them in utter confusion. This was "total war" more than fifty years before its proper time for the devastation rained heaviest on women, children and older folk. To this was added a costly toll in warriors, all of which brought sore grief to Joseph who wished only to go in peace. This was denied him and again he accepted the role his heredity and talents demanded. Rallying the scattered fighting men he counter-attacked, swept Gibbon from the field and left that stricken officer in grave need of help. Such was the Battle of Big Hole.

A strategy of speedier withdrawal now became necessary. For the Indians it was to keep on the move, change horses often, trust to mobility to avoid further conflict with bluecoats. Well-timed feints lured military attention from the intended route which led far south, then eastward through Yellowstone Park. Other "tourists" were there ahead of the Nez Perce and the overburdened chieftain sought to protect them, leaving startled whites with an assortment of tales for children and grandchildren, and in some cases a store of good will which in time would help counter reported civilian casualties, inevitable accompaniment to any war.

During the test imposed by weary months of travel elders faded away, children matured to adult responsibility, boys achieved warrior status and became riders watching for soldiers whose numbers constantly increased. Howard and Gibbon clung to the trail; in Montana Sturgis and Miles joined the hunt. Enemy braves, eager for a chance to raid the horse herd, enlisted in the paleface cause, but not even these odds could prevail. It remained for nature in an unseasonal savage mood, to turn her back and help tilt the delicately weighed balance of freedom or failure. The hope of finding peace in "buffalo country" was blighted for swarming bluecoats had effectively blockaded that route. A short distance north lay "Grandmother" territory, Canada. Sitting Bull and his victorious Sioux had found sanctuary there. Hopefully room might be found for others of the disinherited.

So near and yet so far. In Montana's Bear Paw Mountains the Nez Perce rested. The condition of the harried people demanded it, the exhaustion of their animals dictated a pause for grazing and then a blinding snowstorm enveloped the camp in a mantle that promised concealment while denying the wisdom of travel when wintry elements opposed it. The Indians huddled in camp, rallying their resources for one last push, and soldiers in overwhelming numbers, well-fed, well-clothed, well-mounted, and well-armed, fought their way through the blizzard and corralled everything.

Despair, dismay and desperation remained strangers to Chief Joseph and his followers. They "dug in" and from their rifle pits hurled back the all-out charge which seemed best calculated to wind things up in a hurry and gain commanders columns of favorable press coverage. Wisely, thereafter, a state of siege prevailed, as the Military allowed hunger and the bitter cold to take up the battle. Inevitably the chief was driven to parley with the officers, whose temptation to "hold" him was countered by the knowledge that some of their own were in the hands of the Nez Perce. For a time it seemed that a return to Idaho would follow surrender but everyone realized there would be no homecoming when taunting redskin foes drove away the entire horse herd.

For the defeated it was travel by foot, boxcar, and boat to an alien country, Oklahoma, where other native exiles, the Cherokees, had been sent many years earlier. It was not a good country for Indians from the Pacific Northwest. It lacked the high valleys, clear lakes, pure-running streams, and the ponies left much to be desired.

During the several weeks required to fit this story together Five-Sack saw acquaintances of the early warpath wither and die from discouragement, disease, inactivity, lack of life's normal necessities. Sometimes the stocky Southwest Indians, Comanches, told their stories of conflict with palefaces. Many had been prisoners for years. Joseph remained tall and proud, for he had done what a man must do, nevertheless he appeared worried. On a well-supervised trip "back east" he had gained the ear of "The Great White Father," but there was no sign that urgent pleas in behalf of his tribe were being considered. Though public sentiment was undergoing twinges of "conscience," a lengthy list of Army casualties was also much in mind, rendering the prospect of a transfer to Idaho's rugged terrain or the beautiful Wallowa Valley something better left to the future.

Five-sack, after many impatient months, found his hopes of being sent home at an equally low ebb, but there was a difference: Joseph was bound to his people, Five-Sack was a free agent now that the fighting was over. He began to plan, and stealthily collected or "traded"for certain items; the best bow and arrows available, blankets, a canteen of sorts, dried meat and flour which he hoarded from his rations, additional articles of clothing, spare moccasins and suitable lariat ropes. A steel knife and flint were essential for he did not choose to wait another summer, and without a gun starting fire could be a problem. The assembled articles totaled a sizable pack but he did not expect to tote it far.

When all was in readiness, and immediately after a head count by government officials, the foot-loose Palouse "pulled his picket pin," and snuck out. "The Father's" displeasure was a thing to be greatly feared but the homing instinct was stronger. It was early night, a clear sky plainly revealed the Great Bear and the road lay open. He knew he must travel north and probably west but the present need was to "make tracks," and at the same time conceal them.

It was dawn when, following a beaten trail that tended in the right direction, he came to a spring. Hoofprints indicated that horses, wild game and cattle frequented the place. Tying two ropes together, Five-sack fashioned a loop and placed it in the path, covered the strands well with dust, then retreated into the brush and trusted that some unsuspicious creature would tramp out his scent. At dawn a half-dozen steers, scrawny refugees from an Agency beef issue, came snuffling toward the pool. They shambled over the noose, caught a whiff of something foreign and high-tailed it.

THE SECRET SAGA OF FIVE SACK

Five-sack was dozing when hoofbeats drummed in his ear. A band of horses, probably Indian owned and lean from sparse winter grazing, were following the path. The sun was high enough to show a few tolerable animals and one, a saddle-scored blue roan, seemed the best. When the loop tightened over a forefoot the captive snorted and fought wildly. As the other ponies cleared out another noose was dropped deftly around the animal's neck. The roan promptly quieted, indicating past training.

The Palouse brave was in business. Had he realized that nearly 2300 miles awaited him there would have been no second thoughts. He was kinsman of the Nez Perce whose trails led to Canada, the Dakotas, California and even Mexico. True, there was no recognized trail before him but he would make one. Having watered the pony and refreshed himself it was time to push on, no longer thinking of miles but rather of a safe hiding place. For him night travel would be best, at least for the next several weeks.

A brush-veiled gully offered cover, with grazing for the new mount, but then came an unwelcome snowfall. Five-sack, wrapped in blankets, sheltered himself the best he could. Forced at last to kindle a small fire, he hunched over the flame and munched a morsel of dried meat, which he gnawed restlessly. Fleeing the reservation may have been pardonable, after a lengthy penalty period, but "borrowing" a horse was serious should the owner happen to be a white man.

The snowstorm abated, to be followed by drizzling rain, and Five-sack fared forth. A doubled blanket was a poor saddle for this Palouse warrior who, during round-ups, had learned to favor a rancher's rigging. Perhaps time would improve the situation, meanwhile it was best to leave no sign. There were rills of muddy water to follow and occasional expanses of rock, so the journey continued until near dawn when another ravine offered protection.

Day followed plodding day, monotonously, until at last it seemed safe to vary the routine of night travel. The weather moderated and snowstorms no longer impeded his journey. On clear days the sun beamed from a higher zenith and Five-sack kneed his pony to the left. He little knew when he left Oklahoma and crossed the southwest corner of Kansas. He saw smoke from ranch houses and spent a few nights burrowed in hay stacks while the roan ate its fill.

In Colorado he apparently followed the Arkansas River, but when he gained a full view of "The Shining Mountains" with their mantle of snow he turned north again. Spring had definitely come to this land for the air was fresh and free. Five-sack took stock of his mount. The sturdy pony had actually gained flesh. Its hooves were in good shape, for after the urgency of those first few days any need for concealing his trail lessened. With warmer weather he resumed night riding, letting his horse forage during the day in some secluded draw.

It should have been significant when he entered Wyoming. It was a stockman's paradise, with frequent herds of longhorn cattle, and other groups dark red in color, showing scarcely a trace of horns. There were riders, too, and they carried more guns than the Palouse pilgrim had ever seen on Washington cowboys and perhaps indicated an impending range war. Once the native population was dispossessed the whites sometimes fought with one another, resulting in weaponry being much in evidence. This was discouraging, should it become necessary to swap horses.

THE SECRET SAGA OF FIVE SACK

In a vacant line shack he might locate a discarded saddle or find additional supplies. Some of the chuck that came in tin cans would be most welcome, tomatoes, peaches, and the like; but there were too many guns. It would not have helped had he known how many palefacees were also unhappy about this, with big ranches and small spreads mutually uneasy.

Understandably Five-sack had long since used his original food supply. With bow and arrow or snare he was able to bag small game, plus an occasional antelope. The season was wrong for curing the extra meat. It may be that sometimes a dogie was "slow-elked" and isolated shanties could have yielded up variations in his diet. Continuous travel reduced the rider to rawhide leanness, which benefited the pony, as did the lack of a heavy saddle.

Faring north and west through Wyoming he came to a railroad, the tracks of the Union Pacific. The rattling boxcars revived unpleasant memories, and the much-traveled wagon road paralleling the rails should have done the same. Intuitively recognizing the great "Medicine Path of the Whites," the Oregon Trail, he followed this for nearly two weeks, circling the night encampments of several immigrant caravans.

Five-sack knew he must re-cross mountains for the significance of the Lolo Trail was still in his mind. Actually he crossed the Continental Divide by way of South Pass without realizing how simple that stretch of the journey could be. Then the sight of bluecoat patrols alerted him. Since the Bannock War of 1878 soldiers had been guarding this particular region, which was considered very dangerous for covered wagon expeditions, but the wanderer could not know that. Believing himself to be the quarry he headed north once more, hugging the foothills of a mountain range that offered refuge in case pursuers came close.

Several days of hard riding, during which he crossed various small streams, brought him to a divide. The way was rough and from there he descended to a river, probably either the Hoback or Gros Ventre, with water flowing in the direction he wanted to go. At length he came to a larger stream. In later years Five-sack would declare that "he knew this was the same river that flowed west past his Palouse home." To identify that comparative rivulet with the mighty Snake challenges one's imagination but the Indian acted with complete confidence. Five-sack followed its course, pondering a serious problem. With such a certain guide should he continue by horse or contrive a canoe of some sort?

The question solved itself. Secluded in a thicket he found a long-abandoned cabin. The walls were low, the roof caved in, now entirely unfit for habitation. Once it must have provided shelter for unknown "mountain men," or bewildered members of the Astor "overlanders." Useless, the site yet remained worthy of investigation for near the grove lay a log, roughly shaped and scarred by axe work. Something had interrupted the original artisans and the dugout was far from complete. With knife and fire he set about hollowing the interior but soon gave up in disgust. The wood had deteriorated beyond use. Reluctantly Five-sack turned away and the discovery proved important only in fixing the traveler's mind on water transportation.

Then followed days of riding along the stream with eyes alert for certain trees, or logs partially afloat. Eventually the right combination offered; a pair of unearthed trees, their limbs and roots largely ground away by miles of drifting through rapids, plus a smaller timber, evidently trimmed by human hand, then swept away in a spring freshet.

The discoveries were located over a mile stretch of river and required much maneuvering and tugging by man and horse before they could be floated together. Five-sack had plenty of rope to tie his raft together, the smallest timber being placed in the center. There was sufficient length left for mooring near shore, and he next whittled a tough, green pole to fend his craft from rocks and shoals. With his few possessions snugly packed one primary necessity remained — —FOOD.

The sleek blue roan, unhobbled, grazed close by, frequently pausing to gaze at his master and the sluggish contraption that kept him so busy along the bank. The master stared at the pony, tested his knife and scowled. The blade was too dull! Hacking on the green pole had blunted the edge! Much easier to catch fish or search out a duck's nest when he got hungry. Find a duck's nest at this advanced season? Nevertheless the pony should run free. It was truly a warrior's horse and no Appalousa could have served him better. Only a "digger," always poor and starving, would think of using such an animal for food!

The faithful creature had ideas of its own. When Five-sack pushed his clumsy float into the current and began to drift the roan nickered its loneliness, then kept pace along the shore. Presently a steep outcrop of rock barred the way and the raft bobbed out of sight around the bend. Then the querulous whinny-ing sounded above the rushing waters, fading gradually to a medley of echoes. Solitude, utter and enduring became his sole companion. Though unknown to himself, the tenacious Palouse was embarked on a venture which the Wilson Price Hunt expedition had given up as impossible in their desperate attempt to reach the mouth of the Columbia more than half a century earlier.

On a bright October morning in the early 1880's Wes Lloyd, pioneer rancher of Waitsburg, Washington, widely acknowledged in the Pacific Northwest as "The Friend of the Indians," entered his barn to grain the work stock. When just inside the door he encountered a very solitary and stolid redskin. Mr. Lloyd was never surprised by the behavior of his native neighbors, besides, he recognized this one instantly.

"Howdy, Five-sack," Wes greeted, extending his hand.

The visitor gazed back stonily, then shook his head.

"Me no Five-sack! Me George Lucas (Loo-kus)."

Wes Lloyd was not fooled, but with rare understanding he accepted the situation. Five-sack, for reasons of his own, was "on the dodge," fearful of soldiers. The handshake was completed, and then despite the "new" name, a lengthy talk about "old" affairs in the Palouse village followed. The fugitive continued to "lay low" for years, and only after Chief Joseph and the sad remnant of his tribe returned from exile and located at Nespelem, Washington, did the uneasy brave feel "the heat was off." Then by degrees "The Friend of the Indians" learned in some detail the adventures of warpath, exile, the horseback journey, and more than a thousand miles of voyaging from Wyoming through Idaho into Washington Territory, where towering bluffs along the Snake heralded his approach to home.

Five-sack was always non-committal regarding hazards of the trip but surely it was an ordeal to test the mettle of any man. The raft served well enough but came apart when allowed to drift over the first high falls. Then he "borrowed" a dugout at the next

Indian village along the way. This craft had also been allowed to drift over a waterfall, being too heavy to portage, and shattered on the rocks below. Then followed miles of trudging along the bank until another native encampment was located.

Not trusting his freedom to any man, red or white, Five-sack took advantage of the darkness to commandeer another canoe and a rack of dried salmon. With a feeling of elation he had not known since coming upon the headwaters of the Snake he was ready for the greatest challenge of the entire venture, unfortunately the one about which he was least communicative. If he knew of Hell's Canyon and the perils that awaited there was no hesitation. Years of experience boating among the swirling currents and grasping eddies near the mouth of the Palouse River buoyed his confidence. He may have tried an outrigger, for Owyhees (Hawaiians) had come to the Pacific Northwest with the early fur traders, bringing their techniques and skills. On this wild stretch of river he made his boldest gamble for freedom.

By various means and exertions that defy imagination the journey through the canyon was completed, thus matching the exploit of the steamboat *Shoshone*, which he might have seen in previous years, and whose "crew" could have warned of what was coming. There were periods of balancing warily in the dugout, stints of clambering along the bank or wading as the canoe was eased through foaming chutes at the end of a line. An infrequent "sheep eater" camp invited his foraging talents but these unfortunate natives, all but exterminated, were destitute and went into hiding at his approach. His bow and arrow proved the best source of food when he drifted along, for game near the stream ignored his silent approach. Careful days merged into weeks and Hell's

Canyon, with its perils and pictographs of the "Old Ones" lay far behind.

Along the river scattering paleface habitations appeared and Five-sack resumed night travel, which had not been necessary for the past month. The lights of Asotin meant little to him but a few miles farther on the landmarks of Lewiston, Idaho, brought surges of memory. Many, many moons ago he had helped drive "heap beef" through this area. The steamboats were even more familiar and he glided in the darkest shadows from that time on. Passengers on the big "fire canoes" had been known to use Indian craft for targets. Sometimes the white man's aim was so poor that he accidentally shot the paddler.

Red Wolf's Crossing provided a real thrill. Here Steptoe's men, retreating from Rosalia, had ferried the river, fearful of a vengeful and impetuous pursuit. It was good for a brave warrior returning from the long warpath to have warm thoughts, even though he brought no trophies or other wealth. To the swift current Five-sack added his own efforts. The junction of the Tucannon fell behind, then, long, long months after setting out from Oklahoma, he nosed the dugout ashore at the mouth of the Palouse River. Through the starry night sounded a rumbling salute from that stream's spectacular falls. This and the fretful barking of a late-prowling dog, welcomed him home.

Five-Sack's people were proud of him. They shared their food, listened to his thrilling tales, and maintained secrecy. His white friend would do nothing to bring harm to those who had once owned the land he farmed. Passing years eliminated the danger of arrest and permitted a return to the usual way of life.

Cattle ranges were giving way to wheat fields, which offered no work for a rider, but at the mouth of the Tucannon a small settlement, Grange City, had developed on the site of old Fort Taylor. A large warehouse was built and here goods were unloaded from steamboats. In charge of this establishment was "Colonel" George Hunter. This veteran of the Oregon "volunteers" and the Nez Perce War offered work to the Palouse men. It was hardly suitable for a warrior but Five-sack had little choice. The good hunting was gone and too much fish became tiresome.

While boats were unloaded, or merchandise transferred from storage to freight wagons bound for Dayton, Huntsville, Waitsburg or Prescott, the genial Colonel discussed old times with the teamsters and kept his stoical crew on the job. At least one of those laborers could have "gone his boss a few better" in the relating of personal anecdotes but it was Five-sack's idea of a joke to remain silent. His stories belonged to his people and their very special friend, but he did allow himself a few pleasures.

Five-sack joined other Indians who trooped to the annual Pendleton Roundup. In head-dress fashioned from porcupine skin, plus other colorful garb, he danced like no other. With quills rattling, bells tinkling and feet stomping, it was glorious to re-enact dashing deeds of warfare, especially fine now that Joseph and his people had returned, if not to their homes, at least to their beloved Pacific Northwest. At such times his whoops keened over the packed arena with a realism few understood. Years in hiding were repaid by these occasions when he was a center of attraction.

Inevitably reporters saw in him a prime subject for feature articles. Carelessly responding to a question of matrimonial status he thought "he must have had 25 wives." This should have been a cue that further probings would be wasted effort. Actually he was now somewhat "settled down," though not to that imaginative extent, and served as "medicine man" on the nearest reservation under the title of Star Doctor. In keeping with his past this role had to be varied and not burdensome or confining.

Often he returned and tarried long at the Palouse village, where things were not at all good for friendly Chief Old Bones and his dependents. Life became hard when a railroad was built past Grange City. The "iron horse" hauled all freight and no work was to be found at the abandoned docks and warehouse. The last years were kept from being entirely bad by some Touchet Valley early settlers. Regularly they came in a buckboard loaded with food, especially canned fruit and tomatoes. Five-sack regarded all this as justly deserved tribute which all must share, a splendid treat after a diet of salmon, jack-rabbit and sturgeon.

Relentlessly time moved along. As the Great Spirit granted many, many winters, age increased and tribal kinsmen decreased. Burial ground for the once powerful Palouse nation was a plot of arid earth enclosed by rusty barbed wire. Over it the sand drifted, writhing "dust devels" towered in the brazen sky, and tumbleweeds matted in every fence corner. Had Five-Sack, known also as Five-star and George Lucas, "gone to the ground" there the mighty Snake River could have again dealt kindly with him. Today the tract is buried beneath the waters of Lower Monumental Dam, one in a series of barriers by which civilization is forging shackles on that rebellious stream. A short distance away the oldest of the "old ones," the Marmes Man, lies similarly sealed in his rocky shelter. Instead, when this colorful veteran went to his "long sleep" in the late 1930's he was buried near *Cayuse*, Oregon. Thus fate arranged that a certain true, blue roan pony might also be remembered.

THE SECRET SAGA OF FIVE SACK

During 1945 Wes Lloyd recounted an eventful family history which was prepared in manuscript form. The remarkable story of Five-sack was briefly sketched in that document, and to that extent he "became known," but proper recognition comes years too late. His ancestral village has vanished. Not one tribesman survives! There are no "young men" to glory in the name and fame of Five-sack, *The Last Palouse Warrior*.

F. Sherfey